SAN FRANCISCO 49ERS
ALL-TIME GREATS

BY TED COLEMAN

Book design by Jake Slavik
Cover design by Jake Slavik

Photographs ©: Jennifer Stewart/AP Images, cover (top), 1 (top); Greg Trott/AP Images, cover (bottom), 1 (bottom), 13, 15, 16; Pro Football Hall of Fame/NFL Photos/AP Images, 4, 7; Al Messerschmidt/AP Images, 9, 10; Paul Spinelli/AP Images, 14; Marcio Jose Sanchez/AP Images, 19; Terrell Lloyd/AP Images, 20

Press Box Books, an imprint of Press Room Editions.

ISBN
978-1-63494-365-9 (library bound)
978-1-63494-382-6 (paperback)
978-1-63494-415-1 (epub)
978-1-63494-399-4 (hosted ebook)

Library of Congress Control Number: 2020952633

Distributed by North Star Editions, Inc.
2297 Waters Drive
Mendota Heights, MN 55120
www.northstareditions.com

Printed in the United States of America
082021

ABOUT THE AUTHOR

Ted Coleman is a sportswriter who lives in Louisville, Kentucky, with his trusty Affenpinscher, Chloe.

TABLE OF CONTENTS

PERRY
34

CHAPTER 1
THE EARLY YEARS

The San Francisco 49ers brought pro football to Northern California in 1946. At that time, they were part of the All-America Football Conference. But in 1950, the 49ers joined the National Football League (NFL). Those early Niners teams didn't win any titles. But they did have a big star in fullback **Joe Perry**. Perry was very fast for a fullback.

STAT SPOTLIGHT

CAREER RUSHING TOUCHDOWNS
49ERS TEAM RECORD
Joe Perry: 68

Nicknamed "The Jet," he was the first player to rush for 1,000 yards two seasons in a row. He did it in 1953 and 1954.

Perry was joined in the backfield by halfback **Hugh McElhenny**. McElhenny was a thrilling runner. He had excellent speed and a long stride. He could also catch passes and return kicks.

Offensive lineman **Leo Nomellini** opened plenty of holes for those great backs. Nomellini also played defense. He used his incredible strength to knock opponents on

MILLION-DOLLAR BACKFIELD

In the 1950s, the 49ers' backfield was so good that people called it the "Million-Dollar Backfield." It consisted of quarterback Y. A. Tittle and running backs John Henry Johnson, Hugh McElhenny, and Joe Perry. All of these players were stars. But the group's nickname wasn't actually true. In those days, players didn't earn anything close to a million dollars.

McELHENNY
39

their backs. The 10-time Pro Bowler became a pro wrestler after retiring from football.

Bob St. Clair joined Nomellini on the offensive line. St. Clair intimidated opponents before he even started playing. He stood 6-foot-9 and weighed 265 pounds. St. Clair loved to hit. Fans and teammates loved him for it. He made five Pro Bowls in 11 seasons.

After many years out of the playoffs, the 49ers started to become a contender by the 1970s. Quarterback **John Brodie** was a big reason for their success. Brodie had been with the Niners since 1957. He seemed to get better with age. Brodie was the league's Most Valuable Player (MVP) in 1970. He led the NFL in touchdown passes that season. More importantly, the 49ers won a playoff game for the first time since 1949.

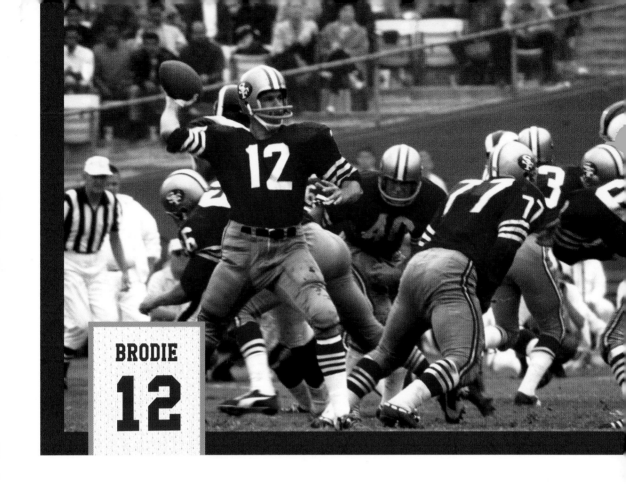

BRODIE
12

The defense was led by cornerback **Jimmy Johnson**. Johnson was an amazing athlete. He had been a hurdles champion in college. His hurdling skills came in handy on the football field. Johnson could keep up with speedy receivers. And he could jump high to swat the ball away.

MONTANA
16

CHAPTER 2

THE GOLDEN YEARS

San Francisco had a few playoff appearances in the early 1970s. Unfortunately for 49ers fans, the team couldn't break through to the Super Bowl. That changed after quarterback **Joe Montana** arrived. "Joe Cool" was known for being calm when it mattered most. Perhaps the best example came during the Super Bowl in the 1988 season. San Francisco trailed with

STAT SPOTLIGHT

CAREER PASSING YARDS
49ERS TEAM RECORD
Joe Montana: 35,124

only three minutes left. But Montana led his team on a 92-yard drive to win the game. He ended up winning four Super Bowls in all. He also won two league MVP awards.

Dwight Clark was one of Montana's top targets. Clark and Montana combined for one of the most famous plays in football history. It became known as "The Catch." The play happened in the conference championship game of the 1981 season. Clark's amazing last-minute touchdown catch sent the 49ers to their first Super Bowl.

THE WEST COAST OFFENSE

Bill Walsh became San Francisco's head coach in 1979. He brought with him an offensive strategy that relied on lots of short passes. This strategy helped set up longer runs and passes. Walsh won three Super Bowls with his "West Coast Offense." This style of offense later became very common in the NFL.

CLARK
87

Offensive lineman **Randy Cross** helped

protect Montana. Cross spent his entire

13-year career with the 49ers. He was there

for three of the team's Super Bowls. Cross did

plenty of blocking for running back **Roger Craig**. But Craig could do more than run. In 1985, he became the first player to rack up 1,000 rushing yards and 1,000 receiving yards in the same season.

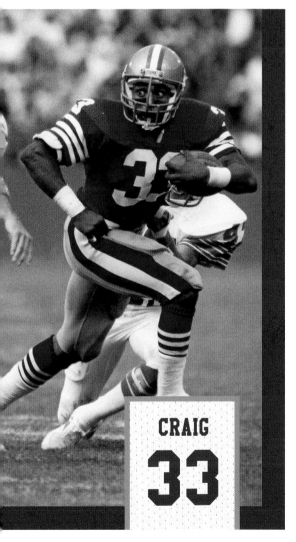

CRAIG

33

The 49ers' biggest weapon was receiver **Jerry Rice**. He had more receiving yards than any player in NFL history. Rice was tall and fast, and he had great hands. He also worked hard on his fitness and on his route-running.

The 49ers weren't all about offense,

though. Defensive back **Ronnie Lott** was a brutal tackler with a nose for the ball. He had the most interceptions in team history. Linebacker and defensive end **Charles Haley** was a ferocious pass rusher. He earned Defensive Player of the Year honors in 1990.

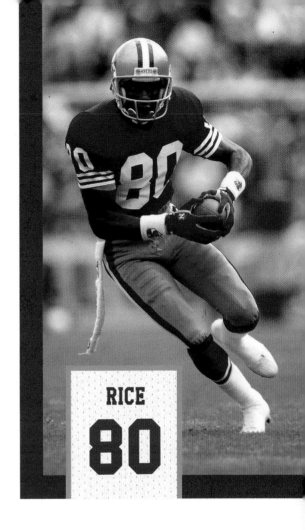

RICE
80

When Montana got injured, the 49ers had another superstar in waiting. **Steve Young** became a starter in 1991, and he was the league's MVP in 1992. Young led the 49ers to a fifth Super Bowl title in the 1994 season.

OWENS
81

CHAPTER 3
THE MODERN YEARS

The 49ers didn't make it back to the Super Bowl until the 2012 season. But they still had some great players during the late 1990s and early 2000s. For example, defensive tackle **Bryant Young** made four Pro Bowls during his 14-year career.

Wide receiver **Terrell Owens** played alongside the legendary Jerry Rice, but he still made a name for himself. Owens played well in the late 1990s. But he exploded after Rice left in the early 2000s. Owens had back-to-back 1,400-yard seasons in 2000 and 2001.

Few running backs have been more consistent than **Frank Gore**. He was only a third-round draft pick in 2005. But Gore recorded eight 1,000-yard seasons with the 49ers. Tackle **Joe Staley** spent many years blocking for Gore. Staley made six Pro Bowls in his 13 seasons.

On defense, linebacker **Patrick Willis** was Defensive Rookie of the Year in 2007. And that was just the start. Willis made the Pro Bowl in each of his first seven seasons. He led a defense that took the 49ers back to the Super Bowl in the 2012 season.

STAT SPOTLIGHT

CAREER RUSHING YARDS
49ERS TEAM RECORD
Frank Gore: 11,073

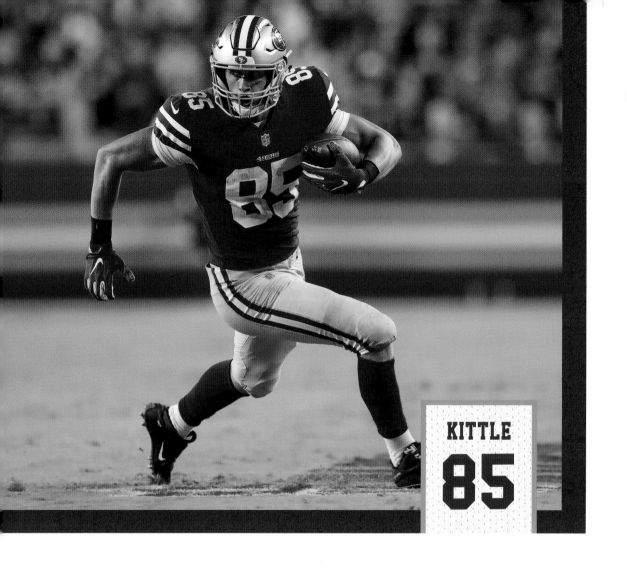

KITTLE
85

After a few more losing seasons, the 49ers rebuilt into a Super Bowl contender once again. Tight end **George Kittle** was the team's main offensive weapon. Kittle was an outstanding blocker but also a dangerous receiver. In 2018,

COLIN KAEPERNICK

Colin Kaepernick took over as 49ers quarterback during the 2012 season. His exciting combination of running and passing skills helped the 49ers reach the Super Bowl. Kaepernick also became known for his activism. In the 2016 season, he took a knee during the national anthem. He was protesting police brutality and racism. Kaepernick helped spark a national conversation about these topics.

he set an NFL record for most receiving yards by a tight end.

Kittle and quarterback **Jimmy Garoppolo** led the 49ers back to the Super Bowl in the 2019 season. It was Garoppolo's first year as an NFL starter, and he threw for nearly 4,000 yards. Meanwhile, linebacker **Fred Warner** was a leader on defense.

In the Super Bowl, he had seven tackles and an interception. The 49ers lost that Super Bowl. But with the young talent they had, fans hoped there would be many more chances.

TIMELINE

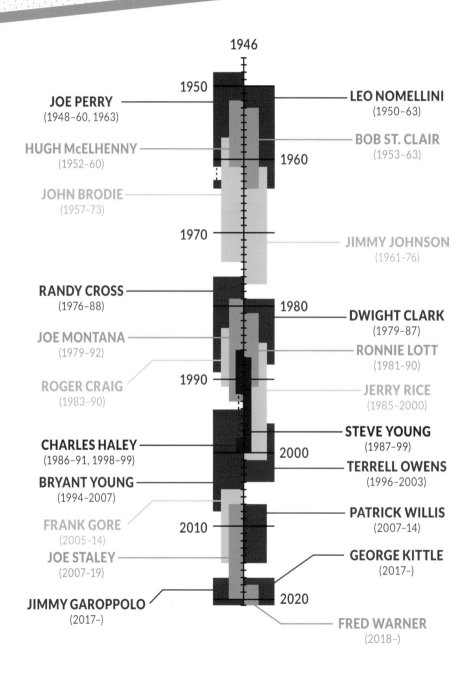

1946

1950

JOE PERRY
(1948–60, 1963)

LEO NOMELLINI
(1950–63)

HUGH McELHENNY
(1952–60)

BOB ST. CLAIR
(1953–63)

1960

JOHN BRODIE
(1957–73)

1970

JIMMY JOHNSON
(1961–76)

RANDY CROSS
(1976–88)

1980

DWIGHT CLARK
(1979–87)

JOE MONTANA
(1979–92)

RONNIE LOTT
(1981–90)

ROGER CRAIG
(1983–90)

1990

JERRY RICE
(1985–2000)

STEVE YOUNG
(1987–99)

CHARLES HALEY
(1986–91, 1998–99)

2000

TERRELL OWENS
(1996–2003)

BRYANT YOUNG
(1994–2007)

PATRICK WILLIS
(2007–14)

FRANK GORE
(2005–14)

2010

JOE STALEY
(2007–19)

GEORGE KITTLE
(2017–)

JIMMY GAROPPOLO
(2017–)

2020

FRED WARNER
(2018–)

TEAM FACTS

SAN FRANCISCO 49ERS

Founded: 1946

Super Bowl titles: 5 (1981, 1984, 1988, 1989, 1994)*

Key coaches:

Buck Shaw (1946-54), 71-39-4

Bill Walsh (1979-88), 92-59-1,
   3 Super Bowl titles

George Seifert (1989-96), 98-30-0,
   2 Super Bowl titles

MORE INFORMATION

To learn more about the San Francisco 49ers, go to **pressboxbooks.com/AllAccess**.

These links are routinely monitored and updated to provide the most current information available.

*1966 through 2020

GLOSSARY

backfield
The players who line up behind the offensive linemen.

conference
A subset of teams within a sports league.

contender
A team that is good enough to win a title.

fullback
An offensive player who sometimes runs with the football but is also responsible for blocking.

linebacker
A player who lines up behind the defensive linemen and in front of the defensive backs.

Pro Bowl
The NFL's all-star game, in which the league's best players compete.

rookie
A professional athlete in his or her first year of competition.

INDEX